Ken Dodd's Butty Book

Ken Dodd's Butty Book

In collaboration with Dave Dutton and Hal Dootson

ILLUSTRATED BY BILL TIDY

M

ISBN 0 333 23282 8

First published 1977 by
MACMILLAN LONDON LIMITED
4 Little Essex Street London WC2R 3LF
and Basingstoke
Associated companies in New York Dublin
Melbourne Johannesburg and Delhi

Typeset by
PIONEER GRAPHICS

Printed in Great Britain by
REDWOOD BURN LIMITED
Trowbridge & Esher

Based on an original idea by Hal Dootson

Book designed by Keith Anderson

Acknowledgments

The authors and publishers are grateful to the following for their valuable help in
the production of this book: The Danish Food Centre, London; The Flour Advisory
Bureau Ltd; The Cheese Bureau; McDougall's Home Baking Bureau; Allied Bakeries
Ltd; Kraft Kitchen Advisory Service; Colman Foods; Van den Berghs and Jurgens Ltd;
Buxted Advisory Service; Taunton Cider Company Ltd; Guinness Superlatives Ltd;
The Dutch Dairy Bureau; The Milk Marketing Board; Sutherlands Foods; John West
Ltd; The Honey Bureau; Mary Hinds (Woman's Editor, *St Helens Reporter*) and
last, but not least, the staff of St Helens Reference Library, Merseyside.
    All references to butter in this book can also be read as margarine.

Contents

Foreword

Hi there funny folk. . . .

The thought may be crossing your mind—what does a mere male like Ken Dodd know about the ancient art of butty-making? To tell the truth, although it's not generally well-known, I've been connected with butties all my life. . . .

You see, I was born and bread in Knotty Ash—and though my teacher thought I was half-baked, I was my mother's pride. Actually I brought myself up, 'cos my dad used to pop self-raising flour in my pram. . . .

At 15, I left school (through the back window) and became an apprentice in a baker's shop—partly because I liked loafing about but mainly because I kneaded the dough. The baker used to send me out on a sandwich course. . . . Ha! Ha! Very good— get off!

Eventually, I found things were turning stale and though the baker thought I was barmy, I left because it was such a crumby job with very little turnover.

I then became a face-worker at the famous Knotty Ash Jam Butty Mines where I used to hack out new seams of strawberry jam with me teeth. I had to give the job up because I gradually came to a sticky end.

But seriously folks . . . the humble sandwich can be as versatile and pleasingly plumpshuss as a gourmet meal—both to look at and to munch.

As a lifelong student and devotee of the Knotty Ash Academy of Buttyology (Buttyology = the study of good sandwich-making), I feel sure that the many suggestions contained in this tattyfilarious tome will brighten up your butties, add relish to your parties and tickle up your tastebuds.

So get your teeth into this little lot. . . .

Ken Dodd, Knotty Ash, 1977.

The History of the Butty

Butties are here to stay—ever since a hungry short-sighted Stone Age caveman invented the Club Sandwich—and broke three teeth trying to bite through it.

Later on, in the time of the Ancient Greeks, Archimedes astonished the locals when he leapt out of his tub and ran starkers through the streets shouting: 'Eureka—I've invented the bath bun. . . !'

The Romans began with butties when they started throwing Christians to the lions between two slices of bread. . .

THIS WAY PLEASE

In Scandinavia, big strapping Viking warriors ran about uttering bloodcurdling yells shouting: 'I'm thor! I'm thor!'—usually after they'd burned their tongues biting into a red-hot bacon butty. . . .

How much easier life must have been in the Middle Ages before plates were ever thought of. . . . In those days, the 'plates' would have been just a big slab of bread which you simply tucked into after eating whatever was on it. How novel! No waste and no washing up!

This bread base evolved into a croûte, which, for those of you who didn't go to the Knotty Ash Academy of Buttology, is a thick slice of fried or toasted bread served on a platter of wood, pottery or pewter.

This delicious device soaked up all the lovely juices from any meats or other goodies laid on it. Thus it became the mouthwatering ancestor of our modern butty.

Such tantalising toasts were the inn-thing from the time of Good Queen Bess and the idea still survives in such scrumptious snacks as Danish open sandwiches, beans on toast and Welsh Rarebit—better known as Big Wanda from the Rhondda. . . .

History has it that the butty as we know it today was the brainwave of John Montagu, the Fourth Earl of Sandwich, in 1760.

He was said to have felt peckish during a hard night's grafting at the gaming tables. . . . Loath to lift his peepers from the game, he popped some best brisket between two chunks of bread and—hey presto! The gamble paid off and the butty was born.

From then on, there was no holding back butty buffs and fanatics everywhere. Anything that was edible—from lamb to ham, from spam to jam—was slapped between two slices of bread and merrily munched upon. Buttymania took a hold.

Over two hundred years later, the butty is still as popular as ever, to the extent that folks in various parts of Britain—especially Wales—affectionately call their best friend their 'butty' (and some even call their butty their best friend. . . !).

Butty Lovers of the World Unite!

(You have nothing to lose but your crusts)

How long will it be before the noble British butty takes its rightful place in the history books?

Do you know, folks, butties have influenced the course of history for thousands of years—ever since Eve tried to tempt Adam with an apple in the Garden of Eden—then finally found his real weakness was for chip butties. . . .

Butties and sarnies have been the subject of misquotations on scores of occasions. . . . Every serious student of buttyology knows what Mark Antony *really* said was: 'Friends, Romans, Countrymen, lend me your butties—I'm fair famished and I haven't had a nibble since V past X this morning. . . .'

And this is the place to put the record straight that what Richard the Third *actually* said at the Battle of Bosworth was, 'A butty, a butty—my kingdom for a butty . . . or if you haven't got that I'll settle for a packet of cheese 'n' onion crisps. . . .'

And can any of us forget that historic moment when Lord Nelson stood haughtily on the bridge of his flagship *Victory* at the Battle of Trafalgar and ordered his signaller to run up the message: 'England Expects That This Day Each Man Will Chew His Butty.' Then he put his telescope to his blind eye and said: 'I see no chips.'

Great buttyologists abound in the annals of history. For instance, there was that famous upper-crust, well-bread French nobleman and part-time chef Cyrano de Bergerac, whose massive conk was the inspiration and original model for the French loaf. . . . He used to go round challenging folk to duels when they laughed at his hooter and he was always shouting: 'Dat's no french loaf—dat's ma nose!'

There was that infamous scourge of the **Butty Dark Ages**—Attila the Bun. . . . There was old Francis Bacon who went round crackling, and invented the Bacon Butty; and of course there was the intrepid Captain Cook who discovered the Sandwich Isles—then ate them for his dinner. . . .

Expert buttyologists know that the *real* reason why Napoleon Bonaparte always kept his hand inside his tunic was because in those days hotplates hadn't been invented, so it was the only way he could keep his frog's leg butty warm when he fancied a nibble in between directing his battles. . . .

And what was the *real* reason for that enigmatic smile on the face of the Mona Lisa? She'd nicked old Leonardo's best beef butties whilst he was mixing his paints—and scoffed the lot down in one!

It's easy to see why the butty caught on. What can compare with sinking your teeth into a fresh crusty cob bulging at the seams with hot chips sizzling with lashings of salt and vinegar . . . mmmmm.

And instead of writing about daffodils, why didn't Willy Wordsworth sing the praises of the traditional British Jam Butty—the thick doorstep wedge of bread, spread liberally with best butter and a lively layer of strawberry jam? It's been the favourite of generations of jammy-faced kids for ages—and long may it continue to be so.

So here's a health unto butty-eaters everywhere in the world. Let us raise our butties high and eat a toast to the man who started it all—good old John Montagu, Earl of Sandwich. Cheers!

Let's Have a Party!

Now is the time for all good boys—and
girls—to come to the lemon-aid of the party

What a buttiful day for throwing a party! Go on—force yourselves. . . . Roll back the
gramophone and turn up the carpet, freak out with yer granny and shake it all about
in the Hokey Cokey—they can't touch you for it, not if you've made the butties.

You don't need any excuse for a party—well, we all have something to celebrate—
such as your tortoise's coming-of-age, the anniversary of the founding of the garden

shed or the fact that it's twenty-five years to the day since you last said anything sensible.

We always have fun at our family parties—after three brown ale ice lollies me grandad is a scream when he does his impression of the Hunchback of Notre Dame with the turkey stuffed up the back of his jumper. Later on, we all love to stand in a bunch round the old upright piano—wishing that one of us could play the flipping thing. . . .

Me granny makes smashing birthday cakes—the only trouble is you can't get your teeth through the icing! In fact she's sold the recipe to a well-known firm of building contractors who use it now in pre-stressed concrete. . . .

Everybody all over the world loves a party. . . . Did you know that at a Greek party, they smash all the plates; at a Russian party, they smash all the glasses; and at an Irish party they smash each other!

I love playing daft party games—like Hunt the Kipper, Bungalow-Bungalow (the posh version of Housey-Housey) and Rentman's Knock (that's where the rentman knocks on the front door and we all hide behind the sofa till he's gone).

You can be too greedy when it comes to helping yourself at parties—I know of one little lad who ate six big helpings of jelly and was set for life.

Once at a party I accidentally sat down on a jelly and blancmange that someone had left on a chair. . . . By Jove I was a trifle uncomfortable!

Us showbusiness folk love a good party, so here are some super sandwich suggestions with a showbiz theme to perk up any party—with some special sweet butty ideas just for the children. . . .

Panto Treats

For Big and Little Kids

Tom Thumb's Tummy-Tickler
Send your taste-buds crazy with canned crushed pineapple mixed with apple sauce and a touch of preserved ginger, spread on buttered white bread rolls and garnished with angelica.

Cinderella's Sarnie
Spread buttered wholemeal bread with chopped, mixed nuts in golden syrup and decorate with glacé cherries.

Idle Jack's Jolly Jelly
Heap a filling of blackberry jelly preserve mixed with desiccated coconut on some buttered wholemeal bread and top with chocolate chips.

Mother Goose's Giggle
Try mashed banana in butterscotch sauce on sliced, buttered brown bread with a sprinkling of caster sugar on top.

Footlights Frolic
Mix finely-chopped celery and hard-boiled eggs with mayonnaise and spread on buttered brown bread. Garnish with a slice of tomato.

Soft-Shoe Swinger
Sauté chopped green peppers and chopped onions in butter . . . add whisked egg, salt and pepper and cook until firm. Serve between cold, buttered toast slices and garnish with watercress.

Wishee Washee's Wallop

Cover buttered white bread with slices of banana dipped in lemon juice, then sprinkled with grated chocolate and garnish with a piece of walnut.

First-Night Fare

Chop hard-boiled eggs and blend with minced, cooked liver in mayonnaise. Season with prepared horseradish, add salt and pepper and spread on buttered white bread. Garnish with a tomato slice.

Spotlight Sparkler

Mix cottage cheese with chopped pimento and chopped olives. Spread on buttered granary bread and top with fresh mustard and cress.

Coconut Curtain-Call

Blend grated coconut, finely-chopped chutney and cream cheese with finely-chopped ginger and a dash of curry powder. Spread on buttered bridge rolls.

Peanut Première

Grind a portion of salted peanuts and add half as much again of grated raw carrot. Blend with mayonnaise and season with a little salt. Spread on buttered white bread.

Savoury Showstopper

Spread granary bread lightly with peanut butter then a layer of sweet pickle. Remove bones from canned mackerel and mash in its own juices with soured cream, salt and pepper. Spread over the pickle layer and top the finished master-piece with onion rings.

Backcloth Baps

Try buttered baps spread with chopped ham and celery in a little curry sauce. Garnish liberally with cress.

Matinée Masher

Meat paste is more exciting when mixed with grated carrot, chopped onion and a

dash of tomato sauce. Spread on finger rolls and garnish with a sprig of parsley.

Beetroot Barnstormer
Place juicy slices of pickled beetroot on buttered brown bread and cover with watercress. Garnish with a big blob of cream cheese.

Slapstick Smash
For a special treat, try buttered white baps filled with flaked, canned lobster mixed with chopped hard-boiled egg, French dressing, chopped chives and salad cream to bind. Garnish with cress.

Busker's Brawn
Put a generous helping of sliced brawn between two slices of buttered brown bread and add chopped raw onion and a dash of Worcester sauce. Top with a tomato slice.

Turkey Trouper
Try an unusual mixture of diced, cooked turkey and chopped olives with Thousand Island dressing and serve on buttered baps. Decorate the top with a little grated carrot and a slice of cucumber.

Finale Flip
Mix cream cheese with finely-chopped spring onions and raw, chopped carrot and spread on buttered white bread. Decorate with crunchy radish slices.

Party Pointers

(For Harassed Mums)

For tots' savoury sandwiches, keep the fillings as simple as possible—use cheese, ham, meat paste or salmon paste. This way you'll avoid troublesome tummy upsets. . . .

Accidents will happen! So protect your carpet with plastic sheeting. This can be rolled up along with spillages and crumbs and thrown away. It also means less vacuum-cleaning for Mum!

Put the plates of children's sandwiches at the edge of the table where tiny eager fists can easily reach them. This prevents little Tommy from leaning over and dipping his tie in the trifle!

Just in case—have a damp cloth, kitchen roll, and brush and pan discreetly handy to tackle little emergencies.

Always consider the toddlers' tastebuds—and only bring out the sweet sandwiches when the savoury ones have been disposed of.

Shape Up Your Sandwiches!

Liven up your party plates by making different shapes out of your sandwiches. Squares, circles, diamonds, triangles and finger shapes all add variety—but that's not all. . . .

Pyramids
Butter and spread several varying sizes of bread circles and stack them one on top of the other—with the largest circle at the bottom and the smallest at the

18

top. You can even vary the colours and flavours of the different layers. These look very attractive on a buffet spread.

Pinwheels

Just the job for Bonfire Night parties. . . . A thin, soft white loaf and a thin, soft brown loaf are sliced lengthways and their crusts removed. The butter and the filling is then placed between the two slices which are then rolled up, Swiss-roll fashion. Cut the roll across into slices—and *voilà!*

Decker Butties

Definitely not for slimmers. . . !
These waist-expanders are made from three or four slices of bread and fillings placed one on top of the other. You can make a stripe effect by using alternate brown and white slices or contrasting colours of fillings.
Simply spread filling upon slice upon filling upon slice upon filling upon slice. . . . Get the idea?

Zoo Snackers

For children's parties, use large slices of white and brown bread and cut shapes with animal-outline cutters. The kids'll go ape on these!

Garnish your 'party pieces' with lots of lettuce, tomato, watercress, mustard and cress, cucumber, radishes, gherkins, grapes, olives, parsley and even cherries. Orange and lemon slices add a dash of colour

Labelling the dishes is a great help to guests (especially short-sighted ones!) and helps to prevent a lot of half-eaten food if they suddenly find they don't like the taste.

Be a devil—experiment with colour and look for tablecloths and napkins that contrast—especially if it's a lively occasion.

Clear away plates of food as soon as guests have finished with them. It can be off-putting for other guests if food remnants are in evidence.

Wash the plates and glasses as soon as you can—it always looks ten times worse in the morning!

Doddy's Diddy Party Games

Here are some games to make your kiddies' party go with a swing—and keep them occupied as well!

Happy Hoboes

Have a hobo get-together. . . . Each child comes to the party dressed like a tramp and on arrival is given a stick with a knapsack tied to the end. Inside the knapsack is a paper bag filled with assorted butties and other eatables. Use the bags to tidy up the leftovers. If it's a birthday party, why not make the cake in the shape of a log camp-fire and get the kids to sit around it while singing 'Happy Birthday'?

After the fun and games, each teeny-tramp is given back his knapsack to take home as a souvenir—but this time it contains a little gift.

The Party Web

This is a great ice-breaker! The idea is to tie small gifts onto the end of lengths of string woven in and out of the furniture. As each child helps to unravel the pieces of string, he gets to know all the others before coming to his gift on the other end of the string in the web.

Merry Models

Here's a great game designed to develop the imagination of the child and still be lots of fun. You simply give the children a large box full of assorted tubs, cardboard tubes, matchboxes, cotton reels, straws, adhesive tape, etc., and tell them to build models—space stations, houses, cars, anything—and give a good prize for the most imaginative effort.

The Island Race

Two or three children race at a time. The floor is the sea full of sharks and jelly-fish—and each child has two tablemats which are the 'islands'. Balancing on one island, they have to place the other in front, hop onto it and pick up the one from behind to move another step forward. This is best run in heats leading up to a grand finale. It can be very exhausting but it's great fun too.

Pass the Parcel
Undoubtedly one of the most popular of all kiddies party games—but remember, if guests are below the age of five, it's best to make sure that there's a little present in *every* layer—and don't forget to stop the music at the right time so that *everyone* gets a prize. Parties are no places for tears!

GOOD GRIEF! IT IS CUSTARD AND SARDINE!

Blind Man's Butty
My favourite game! All you do is blindfold each child in turn and ask them to try to guess the filling in 'mystery' sandwiches. There are no end to the number of fillings you can use here—just have a look through the book!

Thrilling Fillings

Definitely for adults only

Here are two party sandwich fillings that are certain to warm up the proceedings. . . .

Sherry Socko!
Cream two ounces of butter and beat in six ounces of finely-grated Cheddar cheese. Add one level dessertspoonful of mayonnaise, along with one tablespoonful of milk and three tablespoonfuls of sherry.

Beat together thoroughly for a scintillating spread.

Brandy Bopper!
Cream two ounces of Danish butter and gradually add two ounces of caster sugar. Flavour with two teaspoonfuls of brandy and use as a topping for bananas—either cold and sprinkled with lemon juice, or grilled and covered in chopped almonds.

Fractured Fairy Tale

Once upon a time, there was a maiden with the name of Buttyrella. She was so called because she simply just couldn't stop eating butties. Consequently, Buttyrella had beautiful long, shining golden hair, big bright, crystal-blue eyes and a 37-stone figure that'd block the light out of anybody's house.

Now Buttyrella lived with her Ugly Sisters, Aggie and Maggie, and her wicked stepmother in the crumbling, old gothic Greasy Egg transport café off the M1 just outside Watford. She led a fraught and miserable life as a lowly serving wench in the pie and beans department, and her sisters and wicked stepmother used to beat her regularly with broom handles—mainly because she kept scoffing all the truck-drivers' bacon butties when she thought no one was looking.

One day, a gold-trimmed letter arrived at the café. With trembling hands, Buttyrella's wicked stepmother tore open the envelope and gasped in amazement as her eyes beheld inside a royal invitation from the Palace.

It read: 'There will be a Grand Butty Do at the Palace this Saturday night. Be there or I'll smash your faces in, Yours, Prince Charming. . . .'

'Charming!' cooed the Ugly Sisters. 'It's an invitation to the Prince's Panto Butty Ball. Everyone, but *everyone*, who is anyone will be there!'

'Oh goody,' said Buttyrella, munching on a ham roll, 'I shall look forward to that. I fancy a right royal nosh-up.'

'Hah! Over our dead bodies,' echoed the Ugly Sisters. 'If *you* went to the ball, there'd be precious few butties left for anybody else, you overweight barrage balloon.'

And so it was that on the night of the Butty Ball, poor lowly Buttyrella sat sadly all alone in the transport café, flicking cold baked beans at the bluebottles on the wall. . . .

'Oh woe is me,' she whimpered pitifully. 'I *did* so wish I could go to the ball.'

At that instant, the door burst open and in rushed a massive great truck-driver with arms like knotted tree trunks—and a heart of gold. 'Have no fear, dear Buttyrella,' he quoth, 'for I am your hairy godfather and you *shall* go to the ball!'

'Oh—and *how*, pray?' enquired Buttyrella.

'Simple, our kid, just wrap this tarpaulin around you, climb on the back of me truck and I'll drive up to the Palace and tell 'em I'm delivering a lorryload of nutty slack for the boilers.'

'Oh, how can I ever repay you, hairy godfather?!' cried Buttyrella, flinging her arms round her benefactor.

'Just you make sure you're home by the last stroke of 12, that's all,' he warned.

'Why—what happens then?' asked Buttyrella.

'You wouldn't believe me if I told you,' he replied.

When Buttyrella arrived at the ball, she created a sensation and was the very centre of attraction—mainly because she was still wearing the tarpaulin wrapped round her. The Prince Charming made a beeline for her straight away and his cultured regal tones sent a shiver down her spine. 'Heigh up, fatty—I'll show yer round,' said the Prince offering her his hand, which she quickly ducked and narrowly avoided a royal left hook.

Everyone from Pantoland was at the ball. Down the marble staircase swept the most beautiful girl you have ever seen, accompanied by the ugliest man you have ever seen—he looked like a cross between Quasimodo, a wart-hog and an income-tax form.

'Who's that couple?' asked Buttyrella.

'It's Butty and the Beast,' said the Prince. 'And over there by the bar, see?—that's Dick Buttington.'

And she looked towards the bar where Baron Hardup was heartily slapping the unfortunate Dick on his back and saying: 'Turn again, Buttington—it's *your* turn again, Buttington. Get 'em in, me old tater!'

Up rushed Widow Twankee all of a tizzwazz. 'Nicky nackynoo,' she exclaimed. 'Is Aladdin?'

'No—he left half an hour since,' replied the Prince.

Mother Goose was busy avoiding Robinson Crusoe who had his hatchet in his hand. 'You're not getting *me* on a butty!' she squawked, flapping her wings in fright.

Over by the French windows, Buttylocks was arguing with the Three Bears. Said the first bear: 'Who's been eating *my* butty?'

Said the second bear: 'And who's been eating *my* butty.' Said the third bear: 'Ditto. . . .'

And Buttylocks·cockily drew herself up to her full height and said, '*I* have, you great furry freaks. Whaddya gonna do about it huh?' So they ate *her* instead.

Buttyrella could hardly believe her eyes—for on the chaise-longue beneath a potted palm, a large butty was stretched out and snoring away.

'Who's that?' asked Buttyrella.

'Don't you know nothin'?' retorted the Prince, 'that's Sleeping Butty. . . .'

Yes, everyone in Pantoland was at the ball, and Buttyrella was having such a lovely time tucking into the chip butties that she failed to notice the hours were slowly slipping by. . . .

Suddenly, in the Palace courtyard, the clock began to chime midnight.

'Goodness gracious me!' cried Buttyrella. 'It's almost midnight and my hairy godfather told me I have to be in by 12 or else. . . . I must fly!'

So, grabbing a handful of chip butties, she bade a hasty farewell to the Prince, slid backwards down the bannister of the marble staircase and fled out of the ballroom—leaving a chip butty which she had dropped on the stairs.

'Funny woman,' thought the Prince. And as he went down the marble staircase to investigate, his foot slipped on the chip butty—and he did a triple backward somersault, bounced all the way down the stairs and ended up in hospital with a broken crown.

Buttyrella got home by 12, married the truck driver, opened a butty bar in Wapping and made a small fortune.

MORAL: Don't go leaving chip butties on the stairs or you might *not* live happily ever after. . . .

Around the World in Twenty-Six Chews

A Traveller's Alphabutty

Argentina—Gaucho Grub
Fresh bridge rolls filled with corned beef slices, tomato and cress. . . .

'Bully' for you. . .!

Bavarian Stomp
Wholewheat bread covered with slices of Austrian smoked cheese . . . topped with thin slices of raw mushroom and corn relish.

Puts oompah up your jumpah!

Canada—Lumberjack's Snack
White or brown bread, buttered. First lay a bed of crispy lettuce; on top spread a mixture of well-drained salmon, grated onion, lemon peel and natural-flavour yoghurt. Top with a couple of cucumber slices.

A toothsome butty for eager beavers.

Denmark—Ham-Lettuce Soliloquy
(Sorry, Shakespeare!)
White baps, buttered and filled with diced cooked ham and sliced hard-boiled eggs. Add shredded lettuce and grated cheese—then moisten with mayonnaise.

> A Great Dane-ish delicacy.

England—John Bull's Roast of Olde England
White or brown bread, buttered. Fill with slices of roast beef, add horse-radish sauce and top with shredded lettuce and grated carrot.

> A stiff-upper sandwich to beef up your butties.

France—Toulouse-Lautrec's Shorthouse Special . . .
Small slices of crusty French loaf, spread with a mixture of Camembert cheese, chopped pecans, lemon juice and hot pepper sauce in softened butter.

> Ooo la la—try this tasty French connection.

Germany—Kaiser Bill's Big Bite Butty
Pumpernickel bread, buttered—with a filling of liver sausage and sliced, cooked mushrooms topped with a little tomato sauce.

> The 'wurst' sandwich in ze vorld?

Holland—The Jolly Miller's Munch
Wholemeal bread and Dutch butter. Grated Edam, topped with thinly-sliced apple dipped in lemon juice, then add peeled, crushed black grapes. . . . Arrange the quartered slices like the sails of a windmill.

> A delicious Dutch treat.

India—Gunga's Din-Din

Brown bread and butter with a filling of sliced hard-boiled eggs smothered with grated cheese and curry sauce.

You'll warm to this one, missis.

Jamaica—The Big Barmynana Butty

Buttered brown bread filled with cottage cheese and banana mashed with a little lemon juice. Top with raisins and honey.

'Jamaica' nice sandwich?

Korean Kung Fu Chew

White bread and butter filled with chopped pork luncheon meat brushed with lightly-boiled egg yolk and a dash of lemon juice.

Try it—chop-chop!

Lapland—Nomad's Nosh

Rye bread and butter with a tasty filling of devilled kidney spread and onion rings topped with mayonnaise.

The kids'll 'lapp' this up.

Mexico—Tijuana Tuck-In

White bread, buttered. Mix shredded lettuce with cottage cheese and a little honey. Add finely-chopped red peppers (with seeds removed) then use as delicious spread.

Viva ze butty!

Norway—Odin's Revenge!

Buttered wholemeal bread. Chopped Norwegian sild on a mixture of cream cheese and mayonnaise. Add chopped onion, radishes and cucumber with just a dash of American mustard.

A thight for 'thor' eyes.

Oman—Sheik Rattle 'n' Roll's Scoff

Rye bread and butter with a plumpshuss filling of full-fat soft cheese with sultanas, or chopped soaked prunes, or figs.

'Oh man'—what a sandwich!

Portugal—Sardine Supreme

White bread and butter. Mash sardines in

'EE...YOU'RE FANTASTIC WITH BUTTER!'

natural yoghurt and add a squirt of lemon juice then pour over sliced skinless tomatoes.

'Sardine' to please.

Queensland Quickie.
White bread filled with slices of grilled crispy bacon and covered with mouth-watering crushed Queensland pine-apple.

A treat that goes well 'down under.'

Russia—Millionaire's Meal . . . (Or Reds Under the Bread)
Wholewheat bread and butter with a rich spread of raw egg yolk mixed with finely-grated onion and topped with caviare.

You 'Moscow' and try it.

South Sea Surprise
Brown bread with a filling of full-fat soft cheese, pineapple and sprinkled with preserved ginger.

A tropical treat, delicious to eat.

Tunisia— The Chew-nis Chomp!
Brown bread and butter with full-fat creamed cheese topped with chopped dates.

A date to remember.

Ukraine—Cossack's Comfort
Wholewheat bread and butter, with a layer of chopped watercress followed by a mixture of flaked, cooked white fish, peeled prawns and grated lemon peel in salad cream.

A 'steppe' in the right direction.

Vienna—Vegetable Harlequin

Viennese roll with butter, packed with grated raw carrot, cooked peas, onions and chopped celery. Mix with mayonnaise and a touch of mustard.

Waltz off and try it.

Wales—The Freaky Leek

Buttered white bread with thin-sliced Caerphilly cheese topped with chopped raw leeks and grated eating-apple in yoghurt.

A wizard Welsh butty.

'X' Marks the Spot—An X-otic Treasure Island Spread

Buttered brown bread with a spread of avocado pear pulp mashed in lime or lemon juice and cream, with a touch of paprika.

Arr, 'Isle' guarantee you'll like it Jim lad.

Yankee Doodle Dandy—The Wham Bam Hamburger

White bap with a layer of fried, sliced onions, sliced pressed beef topped with grated cheese, sliced tomato and watercress.

It's USA—Utterly Succulent and Appetising.

Zürich—The Yodeller's Yum-Yum

Rye bread smothered in Petit Suisse cheese spread with a topping of crisp cucumber slices and onion rings.

'Alp' yourself!

Open Up!

When is a butty not a butty? When it's a Danish open sandwich—because a 'Danwich' is more than a mere butty—it's a meal in itself.

In fact in Denmark, where they're known as Smorrebrod (pronounced Smerbrer) these bumper butties are regularly eaten with knife and fork for lunch. An ideal open sandwich is a mouthwatering mêlée of flavour, appearance, texture, colour and tastebud tickler.

But where did the idea for this Scandinavian succulency originate?

It all started hundreds of years ago, when hordes of rampaging Danes swarmed onto our shores—and it wasn't for the January sales. . . .

Rowing across the raging North Sea was hungry work for these fierce-looking Viking warriors and as they rowed, they all tucked into their pickled herrings, singing: 'Ours is a nice souse ours is. . . .'

Unfortunately, with so many men on one longship, the galley slave was always getting their butties mixed up—some wanted bacon, others wanted boiled ham and mustard and one or two wanted fresh salmon.

This led to punch-ups among the crew, who had to ship oars and peek into every butty to sort out which one was their own.

Fortunately, one bright Viking lad had the brainwave of leaving the tops off the butties so they could see for themselves whose butty was whose. This stopped all the squabbling and left each man free to eat his own butty before getting on with the business of putting the wind up the Anglo Saxons.

From then on, going topless (the sandwiches, I mean) was the done thing and King Canute became so caught up in the idea he ordered back the waves while he finished his newfangled open butty—and, as we all know, invented the 'wet look'.

As well as open sandwiches, Denmark is also famous for its bacon—in fact when a Dane talks about 'a nice piece of crackling', he's usually referring to his pig.

The Danes are fond of their sagas—they make the best saga pudding in the world.

Then there's Hans Christian Andersen—three of the nicest fellows you could wish

to meet. He used to go round telling the most fantastical fairy stories all the time—nowadays, they call them party political broadcasts.

But above all, the Danes are master butty-makers and they know that to make a good open sandwich, you cut the bread into quarter-inch-thick slices, spread liberally with butter and cover the base completely with whatever topping you care to choose. Then comes the crowning glory of the garnish to add to the appetising appearance. In Denmark, the custom is to serve the fish variety of sandwich first, followed by meat, poultry and then cheese.

Guests usually help themselves using a broad server, rather like a cake slice, and take the sandwiches from large trays or wooden boards. Here are some tasty ideas for garnishes.

Gherkin Fan
Slice a gherkin several times down two-thirds of its length but leave a joined portion at the end where the stalk is. Now carefully press the slices apart to form an eyecatching gherkin fan.

Egg Stripes
Scrambled egg is pressed lightly while it cools. Then when cold, cut neat strips to use as garnish for ham, cooked meats, salami and salad.

Rosettes
For an attractive finish to an open sandwich, pipe mayonnaise in little rosette shapes.

Radish Roses
Keep about half an inch of green leaf on the radish, then slice the radish in sections two-thirds of the way towards the stalk. Place in ice-cold water, and it will open out into a 'rose'.

Danish Delights

With a few British and other Opens

Norse One Cyril

Cover a slice of white buttered bread with sliced liver sausage. Pipe two diagonal bands of creamed potato salad across and stud the piping with little cocktail onions at intervals. Place a piece of watercress each side and a slice of tomato in the centre.

Tivoli Topper

Along one side of a slice of buttered white bread, arrange a row of sliced smoked sausage. Place a row of Samsoe cheese slices on the other side and where the two meet in the middle, arrange onion rings with a tomato sprinkled with chopped parsley in the centre.

Kingsize Canute

Butter a slice of wholemeal bread and arrange a bed of chopped lettuce. Arrange alternate slices of egg and cucumber diagonally across the slice and place a sardine each side. Sprinkle with finely-grated cheese and top with a radish rose.

Tasty Tonguetwister

Arrange two slices of tongue on buttered Danish rye bread, then place strips of rolled scrambled egg across the tongue. Cross this with a strip of aspic jelly and add a tomato splinter to the egg and a parsley sprig to the aspic jelly.

Eric the Red's Spread

Three slices of pork luncheon meat are folded one in front of the other on a slice of white buttered bread. Then top this with a tablespoonful of horseradish cream. An orange slice is cut and twisted and placed on top with a prune on either side. To finish off, strips of lettuce and a sprig of parsley are tucked into the horseradish cream.

Copenhagen Cover-Up

Cover a slice of buttered rye bread with a lettuce leaf and add two tablespoonfuls of Copenhagen salad. Add a couple of slices of hard-boiled egg and a twist of sliced beetroot.

Fruity Cutey

Spread a slice of wholemeal bread with soft butter and lay a lettuce leaf on it. Mix yoghurt or cream with a well-drained fruit salad and top the lettuce. Garnish with slices of fresh orange or banana dipped in lemon juice.

Longship Lipsmacker

Cover a slice of buttered white bread with chopped corned beef and arrange two spears of asparagus diagonally across the slice. Pipe a rosette of full-fat soft cheese each side and top with a tomato slice in the middle.

Hams Andersen

Cover a buttered slice of brown bread with slices of ham and arrange three cucumbers in a triangle. Cut thin strips of rolled scrambled egg and place between the cucumber. Place a slice of tomato in the middle and top with a piece of fresh watercress.

Grape Dane

Arrange a circle of white or black grapes (skinned, seeded and halved) on a slice of buttered white bread. Make a bed of crumbled Danish Blue cheese in the centre and top with a piece of watercress.

Open Sesame

Butter a piece of rye bread and cover with sliced Gouda cheese. Spread this with mashed herring fillet and decorate the centre with a mixture of minced watercress and cottage cheese. Top with two slices of cucumber and a splinter of tomato.

Scandinavian Scrunch

Butter a slice of rye bread and place a couple of rolled slices of ham on top. Prop a pineapple ring between the slices and decorate the rolled ham with mustard and cress. Complete with a dash of chutney mixed with chopped walnuts.

Olaf's Saucy Plaice

Make a bed of lettuce on a slice of buttered white bread and place 1½ ounces of freshly-cooked (but not hot) fried fillet of plaice on top. Pour a dessertspoonful of Remoulade sauce over the plaice and fix a lemon twist lightly in the sauce. Garnish with a snippet of tomato and a sprig of parsley to complete the effect.

Viking's Liking

Place two rolls of sliced ham on a piece of buttered wholemeal bread. Between this, add a mixture of soft, cooked rice and grated apple. Sprinkle this with finely-chopped watercress and top the centre with a slice of tomato.

Chunky Chicken

Heap a slice of buttered wholemeal bread with sliced chicken and ham roll (tinned). Decorate with randomly-placed onion rings and pipe soft cheese into the centre of each ring. Complete with a slice of tomato in the centre.

The Eggo-Trip

Arrange four slices of hard-boiled egg along one side of a slice of bread and butter and place four slices of tomato alongside with the slices slightly overlapping. The centre is piped with mayonnaise and sprinkled with chopped parsley.

Chuckabutty's Chucky-Butty

Place a lettuce leaf on a slice of buttered brown bread. Cut leftover chicken into small pieces and mix with sufficient mayonnaise to bind. Spoon this mixture on the lettuce and garnish with a teaspoon of sweet pickle in the middle and a twisted cucumber slice.

Cheese-Pearer's Choice
Butter a slice of rye bread and arrange a bed of lettuce on top. Crumble Cheshire cheese and mix with mashed cooked pear. Spoon this onto centre of lettuce and top with a walnut.

Shrimply Scrumptious
Butter a slice of brown bread and press a small piece of lettuce in one corner, then pipe mayonnaise down the centre. Drain 1½ ounces of shrimps and arrange them round the mayonnaise. Add more mayonnaise and a lemon twist and garnish with chopped parsley.

Perky Porky
Drape a slice of roast pork on buttered white bread and top with a 1½ ounce mound of pickled red cabbage in the middle. Twist an orange slice and place on the cabbage and tuck in a small piece of lettuce and a stoned prune on each side of the twist. If available, add a piece of crisp pork crackling.

Little Mermaid's Pretty Pickle
Heap a tablespoonful of Zealand salad on a slice of buttered wholemeal bread. Arrange three slices of pickled herring across the top and prop slices of tomato and cucumber slices together between the herring. Sprinkle all over with chopped chives.

Danwich Fanwich
On a slice of buttered white bread, place a small piece of lettuce and arrange three slices of Danish Brie cheese side by side in a fan effect on top. To garnish, top with a couple of mandarin orange segments and a sprig of parsley.

Greedy Gobbler

Cover a slice of buttered white bread with a layer of turkey spread and sprinkle with chopped watercress. Add a diagonal line of mushroom slices.

Cheddar Gorge

Cover half a slice of buttered white bread with a slice of ham and the other half with sliced Cheddar. Cross the two with a row of sliced boiled egg and a sprig of parsley in the middle.

Valhalla Variety

Place a piece of crisp lettuce at one end of a slice of buttered white bread, then add egg slices in two rows along the full length of the bread. Take two anchovy fillets and curve them end-to-end in the centre of the egg rows. Cut an olive in two and place each half on either side of the anchovy strips.

Cheesey Chuckles

Crumble Cheshire cheese and mix with minced spring onion and cream. Spoon this onto a bed of lettuce on white buttered bread and place sliced radish in the centre.

Comic Capers

Grate Cheddar cheese and mash it to a paste with mayonnaise and minced capers. Spread on buttered rye bread and top with a sprig of parsley and two slices of tomato.

Husky Rusky

On a slice of buttered white bread, make a bed of crisp lettuce and heap two tablespoonfuls of cooked sausage meat on top. On one end place half an ounce of Russian salad and at the other end garnish with a tomato slice and a gherkin fan.

British Open

Crumble Cheshire cheese over a slice of buttered brown bread and shake chopped fresh mint over it. Place a lettuce leaf in one corner and in the corner diagonally opposite place a tomato slice with a button mushroom each side. Top the lettuce with crumbled boiled egg yolk.

Roes by Any Other Name

Arrange two slices of canned cod's roe on buttered wholemeal bread. Put a small piece of lettuce off-centre and heap half an ounce of Russian salad on the top.
A slice of tomato and a slice of cucumber are then put together and cut through and twisted and placed on top of the salad.
Cut a gherkin fan and arrange across one corner.

Plunderer's Pick

Put a slice of roast beef on buttered white bread then pipe potato salad diagonally across and place onion rings on each side of the piping. Fill the onion rings with finely-chopped raw carrot and add a piece of watercress in the centre of the piping.

Fresh Air and Funshine Sandwiches

Picnics! Everybody loves 'em—from lads to dads and mams to grans.

Most of us live within easy reach of a good picnic spot, whether it's a stretch of beach, the open countryside or just the local park.

It's fun to frolic in the fresh air with a happy hamperful of beautiful butties and nothing to worry about except accidentally sitting on a hedgehog.

I've always been a fan of pastoral pursuits—ever since I saw a bull chase the vicar round a cornfield.

No matter how popular the picnic spot is, I can always find plenty of space all to myself. . . . I go in the middle of winter when it's snowing!

Speaking plumpshussly, there are several ways of preparing for your picnic. For superfresh sandwiches, you can make your butties at the picnic spot itself with the help of recycled margarine, soup or yoghurt containers which make ideal holders to carry the sandwich fillings in.

Or you can prepare all the sandwiches the night before, wrap them in foil and store them in the fridge.

You can even take your own fridge on a picnic in the shape of an insulated holdall bag—a marvellous modern device which keeps drinks and sandwiches fresh and cool (or even hot if you prefer) for hours on end.

Here's a super tip for saving money. You can make your own insulated picnic hamper by using a biscuit tin lined inside with polystyrene tiles. This will leave you with more money to buy butties with!

Salad keeps freshest in a polythene bag and if you use it as you require it, it means you don't have to suffer from soggy sarnies.

Paper cups and plates are best for picnics—they save both on breakages and washing-up.

Keep sweet foods well covered as there's nothing a wasp likes better than a nibble of someone's jam butty.

Most important of all—always leave the picnic site as you would wish to find it. Don't throw tin cans and polythene bags away—as animals can easily cut themselves and choke on your unwanted litter.

Put cigarettes out properly—costly fires are easily started in summer.

Leave wild flowers alone—they're there for *everyone* to enjoy.

But above all, enjoy your picnic with a varied selection of fun food. I've prepared some super sunny snacks to help your picnic go down a treat. So here we go with. . . .

Doddy's Delicious Picnic Pepper-Uppers!

A selection of thrilling fillings for perfect picnics.

Haversack Happy-Snack
Try crushed pineapple and pear sprinkled with ginger on white bread and butter. It's exotically excellent!

Nutter's Nibble
Cover slices of wholemeal bread with a layer of peanut butter and top with slices of banana. It's nuttily nutritious!

Midsummer Marvel
Use a tablespoon of tomato chutney and one-and-a-half desertspoonfuls of mayonnaise to bind chopped apple, celery and prawns. Spread on buttered slices of granary bread. Deliciously different!

Farmer Giles' Fodder
Put slices of salami or sausage on buttered wholemeal bread then top with cottage cheese, chives and a little grated carrot. Mouthwateringly munchy!

Rambler's Raspberry Relish
Mix full-fat soft cheese with crushed raspberries, lemon juice and a sprinkling of brown sugar, and spread on slices of buttered crispbread. Simply succulent!

Shepherd's Fold
Try a filling of lamb slices, chopped, cooked mushrooms and chutney—with a hint of mint—and spread on slices of white bread. Lusciously lovely!

Granny's Grub
Chop small crunchy pieces of eating apple (Granny Smith's are best) into full-fat soft cheese and sprinkle with mint. Appealingly apple-ly!

Ploughman's Crunch
Grate some Lancashire cheese and cooked beetroot and bind together with mayonnaise. Then spread thickly on buttered granary bread. Chompily cheesey!

Beachcomber Baps
Sprinkle lemon juice on minced pilchards, then cover with grated onion and chopped parsley on buttered baps. Astonishingly appetising!

Anchovies Aweigh
Mix chopped anchovy fillets and hard-boiled egg in some mayonnaise and cover slices of buttered white bread. Eggstra-ordinarily eggsellent!

Forester's Fancy
Onto sliced, buttered granary bread spread an exciting filling of crunchy peanut butter, chopped hard-boiled egg, chopped celery, with a dash of mustard and lemon juice. Crunchily crazy!

Regatta Rolls
Butter bridge rolls and fill with luncheon meat, coarsely-chopped hard-boiled eggs and minced spring onion. Bridge that gap!

Riverside Refresher
Cover slices of brown bread and butter with flaked tuna fish, slices of fresh cucumber and a dash of lemon juice. Tantalisingly tasty!

Turkey Tickle
Fill fresh baps with plenty of butter, cooked slices of turkey, mustard and cress and sweet pickle. Frightfully flavourful!

Sweety Tweety
Butter white bread slices—spread thinly with honey and cover with shredded lettuce, then add cooked sliced or diced chicken. Fingerlickingly fun!

Busy Bee's Bonanza
Mix curd cheese with clear honey and chopped walnuts. Spread on buttered wholemeal bread. Wholly wholesome!

Slap-Up Shrimp Spread

For a really tasty and unusual sandwich, mix mayonnaise with a little curried sauce, lemon juice and seasoning. Sprinkle with shrimps and spread on buttered white bread with a topping of mango chutney or chilli sauce and cress. Dashingly delicious!

Surfer Sam's Snack

Thinly slice raw smoked haddock, add a suspicion of cayenne pepper and a quick squirt of lemon juice and insert between two slices of brown bread. Tastily topping!

Squire's Solace

Pour French dressing on flaked tinned lobster and add chopped radish, chives and seasoning. Bind in mayonnaise and spread on wholemeal bread. Eminently eatable!

Tramp's Tuck

For a simple yet unusual picnic quickie, cover small slices of French loaf with a spread of grated onion and caraway seeds. Tasty twosome!

The Merry Maypole Munch

Gradually add dry cider and Worcester sauce to a beaten mixture of butter and Cheddar cheese. Beat well again and stir in finely-chopped cooked, sliced ham. Spread generously on buttered white bread and top with fresh tomato or cucumber slices. Stupendously sensational!

Deckchair Delight

Finely chop and drain cucumber and mix with prawns into softened butter, then add chopped almonds and seasoning. Serve on buttered white bread. Piquantly prawntiful!

Knapsack Gnash

Mash canned tuna fish with oil from the can and chopped black olives, chopped skinned tomatoes, seasoning and anchovy essence with a little wine vinegar. Serve the filling on white bread and butter. A mighty mouthful!

Fisherman's Fiesta

Remove the bones from canned mackerel in tomato sauce then mash and blend in finely chopped dessert apple, celery, vinegar, with salt and pepper to taste. It's delicious on brown bread and garnished with watercress. Scrumptiously super!

Sizzling Snackwiches

A baker's dozen (plus one) of tasty toasties!

Here's a selection of hot sandwiches to make you glow inside on those chilly winter evenings . . .

Tommy Tucker's Supper
Thickly butter two slices of white bread and fill with grilled bacon rashers, sliced and grilled mushrooms and a dash of tomato sauce. Toast sandwich both sides and garnish with watercress.

Cabdriver's Comforter
Fry strips of bacon, without any extra fat, until they're crispy—then keep them hot. Lightly spread buttered rolls with English or French mustard and place a

stoned, peeled and sliced Avocado on top. Cover the Avocado with grated cheese and place under a medium grill until the cheese is melted. Top with bacon strips and serve immediately.

Bobby's Beano
Toast two slices of bread (one of them on one side only). Butter the untoasted side and spread with a mixture of baked beans in tomato sauce, chopped salami and minced onion. Add a dash of mustard and pop under the grill. When it's hot, top it with the other toast slice, garnish with watercress and serve right away—but watch you don't burn your lips!

Towncrier's Tiffin
Mix flaked tuna fish in equal quantities of mayonnaise and chilli sauce and add a dash of Worcester sauce. Spread on lightly-buttered toast, sprinkle with grated Cheddar cheese and grill until hot. Top with a second toasted slice if required and garnish with cucumber slices. Serve while hot.

Knocker-Upper's Nightcap
Toast two slices of bread on one side only. Mash sardines in oil and add lashings of vinegar, salt and pepper—then spread on the untoasted buttered side of one slice. Top with finely-shredded coleslaw and pop under grill. Cover with second toasted slice and garnish with tomato—then serve piping hot.

Watchman's Warm-Up
For a hot, tasty meal, butter sliced white bread and make up sandwiches with Swiss cheese and chicken spread. Dip into a mixture of egg beaten with a little milk and a pinch of salt—then fry the sandwich in a little melted butter. Cut the sandwich into strips and garnish with a sliver of tomato.

NEWS is A BIT STRONG TODAY!

Midnight Mix

Feeling peckish? Try scrambling eggs lightly with flaked, cooked smoked herring (bones removed!) and a little chopped fresh parsley. Place on buttered brown bread and toast lightly on both sides.

Muffin Man's Mince

Mince left-over meat like chicken, turkey or lamb in gravy, beaten egg or white sauce. Place between two slices of buttered brown bread and fry until golden brown in hot dripping.

Starlight Sizzler

Butter two slices of bread. Mix grated Cheddar cheese with chopped, cooked onion slices and spread on one slice. Top with thinly-sliced tomato and grill. When the cheese begins to bubble and turn brown, place the second piece of bread on top and place under grill. Toast top lightly.

Lamplighter's Glow

Mix chopped chicken breast with grated Cheddar cheese and chutney and spread between two slices of buttered bread. Toast lightly on both sides. Mmmmmouth-watering.

Gambler's Grill

Chop some cooked ham and mix with creamed sweetcorn and grated cheese. Place on a slice of bread and butter and grill until the mixture begins to melt. Place a second slice of bread and butter on top and lightly brown. Garnish with crispy watercress.

Burglar's Break

Place a piece of ham garnished with mustard on a slice of buttered white bread. Crumble cheese on another slice of bread and put the two together to form a sandwich. Fry the sandwich in hot butter until it's golden brown—adding butter when necessary to prevent it burning. Cut into two pieces, top with a lettuce leaf—and eat immediately.

Alley-Cat's Appetiser

For a luscious late-night lineup, butter two slices of bread and spread with a mixture of mashed sardines with chutney and a few drops of vinegar. Lightly toast both sides, then tuck in.

Hot from the Knotty Ash Jam Butty Mines, here's—

DODDY'S DE-LUXE JUMBO JAM BUTTY!

You need two slices of bread from a sandwich loaf; two ounces of butter or margarine; one egg; four tablespoons of warm cherry jam; four tablespoons of milk and four tablespoons of lightly-whipped double cream.

De-crust the bread and beat together the egg and the milk in a shallow dish. Melt half an ounce of butter or margarine in a large frying pan and, dipping both sides of the pieces of bread in the egg and milk mixture, fry both sides until golden brown.

Keep them warm after removing them from the pan and sandwich them together with a little less than a tablespoon of the jam. Top each butty with a teaspoon of the jam and hand-whipped cream separately.

How's that for a jam-packed super-sarnie?

Food Funnies

I say I say I say. . . !

What do you get if you cross a cow with a duck?
Cream quackers!

How do you stop kippers from smelling?
Cut off their noses!

What do you call a vegetable that's just lost its trousers?
A scarlet runner!

What's the only food that keeps hot in the fridge?
Mustard!

What's green and sings rock 'n' roll at the bottom of the garden?
Elvis Parsley!

What's green and goes Byong! Byong! Byong!
Spring cabbage!

What do they call an Indian chipshop in Bombay?
A cash 'n' curry centre!

Where does a baby gorilla sleep at night?
In an apricot!

How does an allotment gardener mend a hole in his trousers?
With a cabbage patch!

Why did the Eskimo stop eating candles?
'Cos it kept getting on his wick!

How do monkeys toast bread in the jungle?
They put it under the g'riller!

Did You Know?

Some phascinatingly phantastical phacts about phood

Did you know that I meself, me, personally, was called upon to slice the biggest meat burger in the world at beautiful Blackpool by the sea in 1975? It's as true as I'm riding this camel. . . . The burger was made by a Bexhill-on-Sea firm for a catering exhibition and had the vital statistics of 4 feet 9 inches wide by 4½ inches deep with a circumference of a whopping 15 feet—and that's a lot of bull! What's more, it weighed a mind-boggling 440 pounds and in trying to work out the calories in it I bust me pocket calculator!

Did you know that apart from the Sandwich Isles—which are now renamed the Hawaiian Isles—there's a Sandwich in Kent; one in Illinois; one in Massachusetts; one in Labrador; one in Queensland; and one in Chile. . . ? With all those sandwiches, it's no wonder the Earth has a crust!

Did you know that in Great Britain in 1976, not everybody was loafing about. . . ? Over 116,000 people were employed in the bread and flour confectionary industry and a further 22,700 in grain milling. And in 1974, the country's output of bread was 2.19 million *tons*—that's enough crusts to give Kojak curly hair!

Did you know that one of the fattest-ever men in the world was appropriately named Cobb? Born in 1926 in America, William J. Cobb ate his way to the record books by achieving the weight of 57 stones 4 pounds. I bet he took some filling with butties!

Did you know that to 'have bread and cheese in your head' meant to be the worse for wear for drink in the 18th century?

Did you know that in 1976, an American set up a burger-eating record by scoffing 17 of them in half an hour? The greedy burger. . . .

Did you know that the jam-butty-eating record is held by a Londoner—Steve Street of Edmonton—who munched his way through 40 of them in 39 minutes on 10 April 1974. . . ? Heavens Preserve Us!

Did you know that bakers' knees is another term for knock-knees—and is said to derive from the fact that bakers were liable to develop knock-knees because of the forced position they stood in while kneading the bread. . . ? Perhaps it should be spelt knock-KNEAD!

Did you know that the reason a baker's dozen is the number 13 is because in former times, the penalties for selling underweight loaves were so severe that the bakers used to make sure the weight of a dozen loaves was up to the mark by adding an extra one?

Did you know that to say 'he took bread and salt' means he took an oath? It derives from a custom in the East when bread and salt used to be eaten when an oath was taken.

Did you know—that even as long ago as 2,000 B.C. the Egyptians were making corn into bread—like a lot of comedians we know? There were about 50 varieties of loaf and their value was so high that officials were paid with them—less three slices for income tax of course—and VAT (Very 'Ard Toast).

Did you know—that at least 660 *million* butties and rolls are sold in the pubs of Great Britain every year? Cheers, me old butty!

Did you know—that the average wheat consumption of Great Britain's population is more than 200 lb per head—not to mention per arms, per legs and per tummy!

Did you know—that to grow a loaf in Great Britain it takes about two square yards of land? This compares favourably with the world average of six square yards per loaf. So next time you see a field-full of fresh farmhouse loaves you'll know what I mean!

Do you know what a bloomer is? Please leave the room the person who said it was half a knicker! No, a bloomer is a long loaf with rounded ends and it gets its name from the fact that the top is slashed several times before baking so that the loaf can rise up or 'bloom' better. So now you bloomin' know!

Did you know—that when the Vikings introduced rye bread, they made loaves with holes in the middle so they could be slotted onto tent-poles for storage? Sounds screwy but it's true. By jove, those Vikings must've been real dough-nuts!

'ONE THING ABOUT ERIC. HE DOESN'T MAKE MANY CRUMBS!'

Did you know—that Stone Age man ate bread that was more like porridge? Yeeeuch! It was made of water and coarse-ground emmer wheat (something like grass!) The theory is that some clumsy caveman dropped a little of it onto a camp-fire but the precious stuff was rescued, eaten and liked—hey presto, the first loaf! After that, a bakestone was used to bake a flat, hard bread . . . which also saved them from burning their fingers.

Did you know—that corned beef butties have now become a luxury? A survey has shown that posh people are spending more than poor folk on corned beef. In the North of England, canned meat sales are more than three times those in the South but corned beef sells only 1½ times as well there as down south. There's more to it than meats the eye.

Did you know—that all breads supply protein for growth and repair; vitamin B1 and starch for energy; calcium for strong bones and teeth and iron for good health? By Jove, two slices and I'm Mr Universe!

Did you know—that no-one went hungry when 25 nuns made just *one* butty for a children's party in Cincinnati, USA? No—they weren't being skinny—far from it. For this Goliath among butties was 7 ft 2 ins long, and filled with 5 lb of ham, 4 lb of salami, 2 lb of cucumbers, 1 lb of salad cream and dozens of olives! The Mother Superior said that every crumb had gone by the time the party ended—in other words, there was nun of it left!

Did you know—that Roman soldiers carried cakes of yeast around with them for making wholemeal bread when they weren't busy mauling the Gauls or bopping Ancient Britons?

Did you know—that a butty burglar made headlines in 1977? Not only that, the 'burglar' had four legs, a tail and a cold nose—because he was Benji the basset hound who became a klepto-butty maniac in his home village of Dobcross, near Oldham, Lancs. After Benji developed a penchant for bread, workmen's butties vanished from site huts and loaves disappeared off doorsteps. . . .
Dog-gone!

Did you know that there's a type of bread known as Lodger's Loaf? Baked in a corrugated tin to give it a fluted cylindrical shape useful for slicing, it is also known as the Pistol, the Rasp and the Landlady's Loaf.

Did you know—that the margarine and butter you spread on your butty contains Vitamins A and D? Vitamin A is important to eye health and Vitamin D helps bone development. So good health and good butty-eating.

Funny Food Facts

Did you know that the sausage butty was invented in 1715 by a German Delicatessen-owner called Frank Furter?

Did you know that the world's barmiest man is Professor Rufus Chuckabutty? He invented a balanced-diet sandwich for tightrope walkers.

Do you know the best way to make a ham roll?
Trip a pig up on a hill. . . .

Did you know that in Britain every loaf is entitled to protection under the National Crust Fund?

Do you know why a slice of toast is the most miserable piece of bread in the world? Because it's always browned off!

Did you know that it's a scientific fact that crusts make your hair curl? Mind you, it doesn't half fill your head full of crumbs. . . .

Did you know that if you rub your face three times a day with a raspberry jam butty, you end up looking remarkably well preserved?

Regional Butty Favourites

Great British Butty Specialities—Who Eats What and Where

Herefordshire folk won't be put off beef, so roast beef slices on fresh white rolls and with lettuce and brown sauce is a favourite.

Sail into **Morecambe Bay**, and more than likely you'll see someone eating a shrimp butty, probably made of brown bread and with cream cheese.

"A GREAT MAN BUT HE WOULDN'T GIVE A BITE TO ANYONE!"

H. McGINTY
INVENTOR
OF THE
LIVERPOOL
CHIP BUTTY

On **Merseyside**, there's no doubt about it. Nothing to beat crispy hot chips on chunks of white bread and butter. You could try spreading beef paste on before adding the chips. And don't forget to lace them with plenty of salt and vinegar.

Over the 'border' in **Lancashire**, they swear by sliced black pudding on crusty bread and with a touch of mustard or mustard pickle.

In **Devon** what else but mouth-watering freshly-picked strawberries on soft white baps and topped with their own clotted cream?

In the **Lake District,** they like Cumberland sausage sliced on rye bread and garnished with apple and onion rings.

Still the rage in **Yorkshire** is good wholesome brown bread with Wensleydale cheese, a little tomato sauce and watercress.

Londoners go for boiled beef and carrot. White bread seems to suit best but it's all a matter of taste of course. If the carrot is raw and grated, and the butty is completed with a smear of salad cream, so much the better for some.

The **Welsh** doubtless prefer their delicious Caerphilly cheese and pickles on wholemeal bread, fresh from the farmhouse oven.

Norfolk has the best supply of turkeys for those butties the rest of us usually only get around to at Christmas, and over there they like plenty of the white meat and stuffing on thinly-sliced white bread.

If you're round **Wiltshire** way, ten-to-one you won't come away without sampling their bacon. And what better way than crackling, fresh from the pan and on finger rolls with a sprinkling of crumbly cheese or cooked mushrooms.

In **Cornwall**, crab butties are usually on the menu somewhere or other. They're best as soft rolls, white or brown and with lettuce and tomato.

Simple fare like crisp butties, condensed milk butties and even sugar butties have yet to sweep the nation from their Northern working-class origins. Ah well, if prices keep going up who knows!

Some Strange Butty Superstitions

Throughout the ages, folk have had some strange beliefs about bread.

More than 300 years ago, a piece of bread which had been blessed by a priest was often placed under the bed of a child as a talisman to ward off any witches that happened to be knocking about the neighbourhood.

Wary travellers along the danger-fraught highways of the time also carried a piece in their pockets to protect them from any evil that might befall them.

Once, it was believed that bread made from wheat which had been cut by moonlight would turn out dark in colour.

In Cheshire, sows were once fed slices of bread for luck as soon as their piglets were born. I've heard of putting bacon in butties but not butties in bacon!

Another belief was that if a loaf was baked on Good Friday, it would never go mouldy and, if eaten, would protect against illness.

The custom of eating hot cross buns on a Good Friday is still with us and this derives from the tradition of eating unleavened bread on that date. . . .

Loaves were marked with a cross by superstitious housewives as another protection against witches (hungry ones?) and also by bakers who didn't want any publicity!

In parts of Lancashire it was, and still is, a strong superstition never to throw bread on the fire, in the belief that feeding a fire also feeds the Devil.

So there we are. Personally I'm not the least bit superstitious—cross me fingers and knock on wood!

Loaf Is a Many-Splendoured Thing!

What's a butty without bread I always say . . . if it wasn't for the bread, it'd be all middle and no outsides.

That's why we, that is *us* at the Knotty Ash Academy of Buttyology are always at the forefront of futuristic scientific advances in the cause of better butties and space-age loaf technology.

Night and day, the delicious niff of freshly-baked bread wafts temptingly around our Loaf Research Laboratories as the finest boffin bakers and crust technicians in the world experiment with new types of bread to tickle your tastebuds.

Of course, it's all under wraps and very hush-hush at present, but here are some half-baked ideas for barmy breads of the future.

Clockwork Cobs. Wind them up and they bounce up and down dunking themselves in the gravy as they go.

The Musical French or German Loaf. To wake you up at the breakfast table, it plays 'Kitten on the Keys' by Depussy and the 'Crumpet Voluntary'.

Stayfresh Bread. It lasts for 25 years, then qualifies for a pension from the Post Office.

The Portable Television Loaf. The only loaf to receive transmissions from the BBC— the British Breadcasting Corporation. . . .

The Floating Viennese Loaf. Hums snatches of Strauss and keeps you company in the bath.

Fireproof Sliced Bread. Stops the toast from catching fire.

The Anti-Theft Woof-Woof Patent Barking Loaf. For frightening away butty burglars— it barks like an alsatian dog when you pick it up.

The Solar Energy Loaf. Can only be eaten on a Sun-day.

THEY **WILL** CALL ME WONDERLOAF

Elastaloaf. The world's first stretch bread—you can exercise with it as you eat it, and use it as a chest expander.

Hinged Sliced Bread. It saves you having to fold your butties in the middle. What a time-saver!

Not to mention our associate projects like Dial-a-Duff, Whistling Rissoles, Yodelling Muffins, Bionic Baps and Computer Pasties (they tell you when you've had enough). As chief butty-tester, there's nothing I like better than to sink me teeth into a nice freshly-baked crusty piece of bread—and I've got the teeth for the job, I can tell you. They just crumble away—your teeth not the bread. However, if you simply just can't wait to try out our Space Age sarnies, here are some superb and unusual bread recipes to be going on with:

Bready? Steady? Go. . . .

Tipsy Rolls
(Try this sway.)

You'll need four soft rolls, half-an-ounce of butter, one thinly-sliced onion or leek, three ounces of grated Cheddar cheese, one grated carrot, one beaten egg, half a pint of dry cider (reduced to a quarter of a pint by boiling in a pan), a pinch of garlic powder and salt and pepper to taste.

Method: Melt the butter and lightly fry leek or onion. Cut a thin slice from the top of each roll and keep to one side. Remove the bread from inside the rolls and soak this in cider. Add the leek or onion, carrot, egg, cheese, garlic powder and seasoning and mix thoroughly. Divide this mixture between four empty bread rolls and replace the 'lids'. Wrap the rolls in aluminium foil and bake

in an oven heat of 190 deg. C. (375 deg. F.), gas mark five, for about fifty minutes. The four Tipsy rolls are delicious served hot or cold—hic! Exshcuse me, I simply musht have another one. . . .

Ribbon Loaf
(S'nice to slice.)

You'll need one white and one brown tin loaf (uncut), four ounces of softened butter, two ounces of grated Swiss or Cheddar cheese, one jar each (one-and-a-quarter-ounce size) of chicken or turkey spread, sardine spread and crab spread, a small, thinly-sliced crisp eating apple, two ounces of finely-chopped walnuts or almonds, two ounces of roughly-chopped black olives, eight ounces of softened cream cheese and watercress, pimento and peanuts to decorate.

Method: Take the crusts from the bread and cut each loaf lengthwise into thin slices. Butter each slice thinly. Combine the grated cheese and apple with the chicken spread, the olives with the sardine spread and the chopped nuts with the crab spread. Layer the slices of bread with fillings, ending with a slice buttered-side down. Smear the whole loaf with cream cheese and chill for a couple of hours. Decorate this with a large 'flower' comprised of cress for the stem and leaves and a head of pimento curl with peanut petals. The recipe provides for six servings when the loaf is sliced. It's a real blue ribbon butty.

Flowerpot Loaf
(Bill and Ben's Treat.)

You'll need half a pound of brown flour, half a pound of plain white flour, two level teaspoons of granulated sugar, half an ounce of butter, half an ounce of fresh yeast, a quarter of a pint of lukewarm milk, a quarter of a pint of lukewarm water. Small quantity of Sesame seeds.

Method: Sift the flours, sugar and salt into a mixing bowl, and rub in the butter finely. With a little of the warm water mix the yeast to a smooth and creamy liquid then blend in the rest of the water and milk. Add to dry ingredients and mix to a fairly soft dough making sure the sides of the bowl are left clean. Turn on to a flour-dusted board and knead for about ten minutes until smooth. Place the dough into a greased clay flowerpot about six inches wide at the top. Divide the top into five by making five half-inch-deep cuts on the surface. Sprinkle the dough with Sesame seeds and cover with a damp tea towel. Leave in a warm place until double in size. Mark again, then bake in a hot oven—220 deg. C. (425 deg. F.), gas mark seven, for about 35 minutes. Turn out and cool on a wire rack.

Slobbadobbalop! (*Translation:* It's one for the pot!)

The Lucky Horseshoe
(A sure winner.)

You'll need one long French loaf, two ounces of butter, six ounces of Cheshire cheese, and the head of one celery and a touch of paprika.

Method: With a sharp knife, cut the loaf almost through into ten even pieces. Spread butter on the cuts. Cut ten wedge-shaped pieces of cheese and insert one wedge into each slit. Start at one end of the loaf and work along. As you do so it will form itself into a horseshoe shape. Sprinkle lightly with paprika. Scrub the celery and arrange celery sticks in a small container in the centre of the horseshoe. This is a butty bound to 'gee up' any party!

Finger Rolls
(A pointer to good eating.)

You'll need (to make about two dozen) one pound of flour—warmed and sieved—a quarter of an ounce of salt, one ounce of butter or margarine, a couple of eggs, an ounce of sugar, a quarter to half pint of milk, one-and-a-half ounces of yeast and a little beaten egg and salt to glaze.

Method: Heat the milk and dissolve the butter in it, allowing it to cool to blood heat. With a little of the sugar cream the yeast, then beat the eggs, adding the warm milk. Next, sift the flour and salt, add the remaining sugar and make a well to add the liquids. After mixing thoroughly, knead then leave to rise for about an hour. Lightly knead again and shape into small fingers. Arrange them fairly close together on greased baking sheets and brush over with the beaten egg and salt. Cover with a damp cloth and leave for about half an hour to rise again. Brush over again and bake in the centre of a hot oven (440 deg. F.) Gas mark eight for about 20 minutes.

Lots of fingers always come in handy!

Party Bread
(This one's a cracker.)

You'll need one large French loaf, four ounces of butter, three-quarters-of-a-pound of minced beef, one chopped onion, four tomatoes, 10 thin slices of Dutch Gouda cheese (about six ounces), three ounces of breadcrumbs, two tablespoons of tomato purée, salt, pepper and nutmeg and a pinch of mixed herbs.

Method: Slice the bread in half lengthways and scoop out the middle. Melt two ounces of the butter and brush inside the scooped-out loaf with the melted butter. Melt the remaining two ounces of butter in a frying pan and cook the minced beef and onion for ten minutes. Add tomato purée, breadcrumbs, herbs and seasoning. Place the slices of cheese in the scooped-out loaf, allowing them to overlap the sides. Now fill the cheese and bread with the meat mixture and place in the oven at about 179 deg. C. (350 deg. F.), gas mark four, for between 15 and 20 minutes. Decorate with sliced tomato and wedges of Gouda cheese before serving hot.

It's my favourite party piece.

Soda Bread
(Dandy with brandy?)

You'll need one pound of plain white flour (or white and wholemeal mixed), two teaspoons of bicarbonate of soda, one teaspoon of salt, one ounce of fat, four teaspoons of cream of tartar and about half a pint of milk.

Method: Sift the flour, soda, salt and cream of tartar into a mixing bowl. Rub in the fat and add enough milk to make a soft dough. Turn the mixture on to a floured board and knead lightly for about a minute. Next, shape into a round and put on to a greased baking sheet. Make three deep diagonal cuts across the top and place in the oven at 220 deg. C. (425 deg. F.), gas mark seven. Leave for about three-quarters-of-an-hour until well-raised, lightly-browned and quite firm underneath. Buttermilk or sour milk may be used but, if so, the cream of tartar should be cut down to two teaspoons.

No need to splash out on this one!

Samsoe Cheese Bread
(Our Sam's-so keen on this.)

You'll need 12 ounces of plain flour, a quarter of a pound of Samsoe cheese (grated), one ounce of finely-chopped onion, one ounce of lard, half an ounce of fresh yeast, one beaten egg, seven fluid ounces of water, a quarter of a level teaspoon of mixed herbs and half a 50 mg ascorbic acid tablet.

Method: First blend the yeast, water and ascorbic acid tablet. Rub the lard into the flour, adding three ounces of the grated cheese, salt, sugar, onions and herbs.

Mix well then pour on the yeast liquid and mix again to form a dough. Turn the mixture out onto a flour-dusted board and knead for about 10 minutes. When smooth, shape into a ball and place in a lightly-oiled polythene bag. Leave this to stand in a warm place for at least five minutes.

Now divide the dough into three and roll each piece into a 12-inch-long strip and join pieces at one end with a little beaten egg. Place the dough on a floured baking sheet, plait loosely and seal the end with egg.

Place the loaf and baking sheet inside an oiled polythene bag and leave in a warm place again until the dough is double in size. This takes about 40 minutes. Remove from the bag, brush with egg and sprinkle with the remaining cheese. Cook in the centre of a fairly hot oven—204 deg. C. (400 deg. F.), gas mark six, for about 25 minutes. When cooled spread with butter and serve.

You'll never be cheesed off with this. . . .

Bath Buns

(These should plug the hunger gap.)

You'll need one pound of plain flour, a quarter of a pound of butter or margarine, one ounce of yeast, a teaspoonful of salt, a quarter of a pound of sugar, half a pint of lukewarm milk, three eggs, two ounces of finely-chopped candied peel, two ounces of sultanas and a little grated lemon rind.

Method: The flour and salt are sifted together before rubbing in the fat. Put to warm, then cream the yeast with a teaspoonful of the sugar. Beat the eggs, then make up to half a pint with the warm milk before adding this to the creamed yeast. Pour into the

flour and beat by hand for about five minutes. Now cover and leave in a warm place until the dough has doubled. Use a flour-dusted board on which to knead the mixture, mixing in the remainder of the sugar, lemon rind, peel and sultanas. Mould into 12 buns, place on greased baking trays and leave in the warmth for another half an hour. Brush with a little sugar dissolved in water and sprinkle with coarse sugar before baking for 20 minutes in a fairly hot oven—204 deg. C. (400 deg. F.), 'gas mark six.

But don't eat too many or you'll sink in the bath!

Pan-try Loaf
(This really means try a pan.)

You'll need one pound of plain flour, two ounces of soft butter, half a pint of yoghurt or sour milk, one level teaspoon each of bicarbonate of soda, salt and cream of tartar.

Method: The dry ingredients are sieved into a mixing bowl and the butter rubbed in. Next, add the yoghurt or sour milk and mix to a dough. Grease a 12-inch frying pan and, having made the dough into a large patty, place it in the pan and cook for about half-an-hour on a medium heat. It's best to cut the patty into quarters and turn these occasionally.

If at first you don't succeed, fry, fry again. . . .

Doddy's Butty Tips

Sandwich bread should be about 24 hours old. The reason? New bread is often very difficult to slice without crumbling it to pieces—so don't get fresh. . . !

Warming the blade of your bread-knife by dipping it in hot water makes unsliced bread a lot easier to cut—and also stops your butties from catching colds!

A great way to keep bread fresh is to take a potato, wash and dry it and keep it by your bread in the bread bin—be thankful for small murphies!

Unwrapped sandwiches will remain fresh for about 30 minutes at an average room temperature of about 70 degrees—after that, the bread starts to dry out and become hard. So keep one eye on the clock, one eye on your butties and the other on your guests!

A pound of grated cheese will normally fill around 15 normal-size sandwiches—or one *big* one if you're a real greedyguts!

Buttering bread acts as a waterproof barrier and prevents moist fillings from going through the bread. As a rule, about half a pound of butter or margarine will cover 30 slices of a standard-size loaf—so do a good cover-up job!

When making butties in advance for a party, wrap them in polythene bag or aluminium foil and pop them in the fridge or keep them in a cool place until they are needed— stay cool man!

If you are making lots of sandwiches, try slicing the bread lengthways and chopping it up into butties—it saves energy and slices the time in half.

Stale bread can be freshened up by dipping the whole loaf under running cold water for a couple of minutes and putting it into a slow oven for 45 minutes or so and it comes out smelling crusty and tasting fresh as new—but don't try it with ice-cream!

Cold water poured over hard-boiled eggs before shelling prevents a black ring from appearing round the yolk—and it's good for shifting the black ring round little Johnny's neck as well!

Eggs stored with the pointed ends uppermost don't keep as fresh as when stored the other way round—and they fall over a lot more too!

Wrapping sandwiches in lettuce leaves before packaging keeps them fresher and prevents tainting by the flavours of the paper—'lettuce' hope you think it's a good idea!

Use leftover sandwiches to make breadcrumbs for coating fried foods. Stale bread should be crumbled and spread onto a baking sheet and put into the oven while you're using it for something else. Place the baked crumbs between two sheets of greaseproof paper and roll with a rolling-pin, then store in a sealed jar until needed—oh what a crumby idea!

The crustiest breads have been baked on oven-bottoms—so look out for loaves with crusty bottoms!

If you have any cheese left over at parties, grate all the pieces together, mix with a little cooking wine, creamed butter and black pepper; cover with melted butter and use as a spread later—what a grate idea!

Never serve cheese or eggs straight from the fridge. You'll notice there's more flavour in the cheese if it has been at room temperature for a while and your eggs will be less likely to crack—thaw thaw quick quick thaw!

Vinegar used in the weekly rinsing of the bread-bin will discourage the formation of mould—and it's smashing on chips as well!

A good crust can be achieved on a tin-loaf if it is baked for longer than the specified time—it's a cracking tip!

Sandwiches made from very thin bread look daintier if the crusts are removed; but large sandwiches keep better if the crusts are left on—we'll crust that one when we come to it!

To crisp up your salad-sandwich lettuce, wash it under running cold water, drain and shake gently in a clean dry cloth. Enclose it lightly in some foil and pop it into the fridge for an hour before putting it on your butties—what a crisp thought!

The best lemons are the ones that are thin-skinned and shiny. Drop them into boiling water before squeezing and you will extract every last drop of the juice—'juicy' what I mean?

How do you make a butty last for weeks? Freeze it—butties can last for up to eight weeks in the freezer, provided they aren't filled with egg or dairy-based products. Remove the crusts and wrap in foil or waxed paper. Once defrosted, sandwiches should be eaten almost immediately—'freezer' jolly good fellow!

For a crusty topping finish to your bread, brush the tops of loaves with salt and water, sprinkle with cornflakes and return to the oven to bake for a few extra minutes—sounds corny but it works!

Make your butties more exciting with the 'hard and soft' technique. Try contrasting something crisp and crunchy—like chopped celery, lettuce, nuts, apple, carrot, watercress or potato crisps with cream cheese, pâté, fish, honey or chicken—it's crunchable and munchable!

Here's a mouthwatering tip for cast-off crusts. Dip them into melted butter and smother them with grated cheese, then pop them in a fairly hot oven until they are golden—and crunchy—calorifically terrific!

Making a few?

When making up sandwiches, remember that. . . . One large loaf (28 ounces) will give you between 20 and 24 slices. A small one (14 ounces) will divide into between 10 and 12 slices.

From a long sandwich loaf of 3½ lbs weight, you should get about 50 slices.

Some more useful quantities: A quarter-of-a-pound of creamed butter will do for 10 to 12 sandwiches and half a pound will cover 24 bread rolls.

The following should be enough for eight sandwiches: six hard-boiled eggs mixed with mayonnaise; half a pound of cooked meat (thinly-sliced); four ounces of grated cheese mixed with pickle; or one seven-ounce can of salmon mixed with mayonnaise.

★★

Bake-a-Butty!

Bet you didn't know you could bake a butty. Here's how. They can be open, closed or rolled and if you brush the outer surface of the bread with melted butter before baking, they'll be extra crispy. For a drier texture, leave them plain. Then all you have to do is bake for about 15 minutes in a hot oven at 220 deg. C. (424 deg. F.), gas mark seven.

★★

Their Fame Is Spreading

Whenever I come across something good 'n' tasty, I always believe in spreading it around. Here is a selection of super spreads to give your butties extra toothsomeness.

Funnion: Use two ounces of soft butter or margarine, one ounce of chopped cooked chicken; one chopped cooked onion and one ounce of chopped cooked ham. Liquidise and spread as required.

Tuna-Tom: Use a three-and-a-half-ounce can of tuna fish, three tablespoons of tomato ketchup and one teaspoon of vinegar. Mix thoroughly and spread.

Azbeans: Use one small can of baked beans, three ounces of grated cheese and black pepper to taste. Mash with a fork until smooth, spread as required.

Scrumpycrumble: Use 12 ounces of finely-grated Cheddar cheese; two ounces of soft butter or margarine; two ounces of finely-chopped cooked ham; a quarter pint of dry cider and a teaspoon of Worcester sauce. First blend the butter and the cheese; gradually add the cider and sauce— mixing well—then finally stir in the ham. . . .

Sardine Scoop: Use one can of drained and boned sardines; two ounces of soft butter or margarine; one teaspoon of curry powder and one teaspoon of lemon juice. Mix thoroughly and spread.

Cornucopia: Use two ounces of finely-chopped corned beef; two ounces of soft butter or margarine, two tablespoons of sweet pickle or chutney; one tablespoon of tomato ketchup and one teaspoon of meat extract. Mix well together and spread.

Pepperpicker: Use one ounce of grated Cheshire cheese; a chopped lettuce leaf; a quarter of a red pepper and two ounces of soft butter or margarine. Mix thoroughly and spread.

Blue-Belter: Use two ounces of Danish Blue cheese; two ounces of soft butter or margarine; one tablespoonful of lemon juice and a little black pepper to taste. Blend and spread.

Pinetopper: Use one small carton of cottage cheese, two tablespoons of crushed pineapple and pepper to taste. Mix thoroughly and spread.

Hentertainer: Use one hard-boiled egg (chopped), two ounces of soft butter or margarine; half a tablespoon of salad cream and a little chopped parsley. Blend and spread.

Gingeroo: Use one small packet of cream cheese, two teaspoons of stem ginger (finely-chopped) and one teaspoon of ginger syrup. Blend and spread.

Milky Wha-Hay! Use a small can of condensed milk, one egg yolk and the rind and juice of a lemon. Beat the lot together and leave for a couple of hours to set, or you can cook it for about ten minutes in a basin over boiling water until it has thickened. Stir well.

Apple Cor! Use half a medium-sized apple, which you then peel and grate, then take two ounces of cottage cheese; two ounces of soft butter or margarine and mix thoroughly and spread.

Shrimpathy Spread: Use two ounces of peeled shrimps; a small quantity of watercress; two ounces of soft butter or margarine and a dash of lemon juice. Blend and spread.

Here's one that should go down a treat with the kids. . . .

Coco's Corker: Use two ounces of margarine, four tablespoons of cocoa powder, two tablespoons of condensed milk, one tablespoon of black treacle and a few drops of orange or vanilla essence or one drop of peppermint or rum essence. Mix thoroughly and spread.

Tempt 'Em

Spread-it-yourself parties are great fun and as there is little or no last-minute rush in the preparation you can greet your guests looking cool, calm and collected.

For extra effect, deck up a tray and have the spreads in different-coloured pots with each spread garnished to attract and tempt your guests. A small bowl of salad on the tray will make it even more appetizing.

Don't forget to provide a variety of fresh crusty breads, chunks of French bread, crispbreads and toast.

If you enjoy eating spreads but haven't the time to make them up yourself, it's easier and quicker to make use of the many excellent brand-name spreads readily available at your corner shop. Keep a supply of these in your kitchen cupboard and you're always ready for surprise guests.

Spreads and pastes are just the thing to add zest to other butty ingredients. So— spread it around!

The Who's Who of Buttyologists

Everyone, from the beginning of Coronation Street to the end of the Strand has a favourite butty. Here is just a crust-section of the celebrities I have interviewed.

Golf pro I.N.A. Bunker told me: 'I like a jam butty with my tee, but right now I'm feeling under par—I'll settle for a club sandwich. . . .' Bunker, you will recall, was the winner of the Danish Open.

Cricketing ace N.O. Ball spoke to me off his own bat: 'I like the sweet butties—savoury ones seem to crease me,' he commented. 'But I'm usually stumped for ideas anyway.' Never mind—this book should bail him out!

20-stone international soccer star I. Cloggem can't leave chip butties alone. The only trouble is if he stokes up with too many before the big match, it keeps his centre forward and he can't see the ball! He confessed: 'I'm thinking of kicking them into touch.'

A man who backs it both ways, however, is that jovial jockey Ivor Stirrup, famous for his win on the thoroughbread Bread Bun in the Grand National. He quipped: 'I have so many apple butties before the start of a race I usually end up stalled before being pipped at the post.'

It was when I was called to the bar—at my local in Knotty Ash—that I bumped into the Master of the Rolls, Mr Justice Wigg-On. Asked for his butty verdict in one sentence, he summed it up this way: 'Briefly, it's all a case of trial and error but I do like a stab at the pickles. Case dismissed!'

Exhaustive tests of varous spreads have been made by international racing driver Monty Carlow. 'We always rally round the butty table. . . . I lap 'em up and they stop me from getting tyred,' he said, before zooming off down the road.

Last word from the toast of Swansea, the barmy bard Dai Gress. After winning the Eistedfood, he said poetically:

> *Leek's a lovely filling*
> *On top of peanut butter*
> *But if I harp on about it*
> *You'll think that I'm a nutter!*

Read All About It

Little Tommy Tucker
Sings for his supper;
What shall we give him?
White bread and butter.

Tommy Thumb's Pretty Song Book (c. 1744)

'A loaf of bread,' the Walrus said,
'Is what we chiefly need:
Pepper and vinegar besides
Are very good indeed—
Now if you're ready, Oysters dear,
We can begin to feed.'

Lewis Carroll (1832–1898), *Through the Looking Glass*,
ch. 4. 'The Walrus and the Carpenter'.

'Heads, heads. . . ! . . . five children—mother—tall lady, eating
sandwiches—forgot the arch—crash—knock—children look round—
mother's head off—sandwich in her hand—no mouth to put it in—
head of a family off— shocking, shocking!'

Charles Dickens (1812–1870), *Pickwick Papers*,
ch. 2. Jingle is speaking.

'No bread. Then bring me some toast!'

Punch, vol. xxiii, p. 18, 1852.

80

Bachelor's fare; bread and cheese, and kisses.

> Algernon Charles Swinburne (1837–1909), *Polite Conversation,* Dialogue 1

The lion and the unicorn
Were fighting for the crown;
The lion beat the unicorn
All around the town.
Some gave them white bread,
And some gave them brown;
Some gave them plum cake,
And sent them out of town.

> In William King, *Useful Transactions in Philosophy* (1708–9)

Give to me the life I love,
Let the lave go by me,
Give the jolly heaven above
And the byway nigh me.

Bed in the bush with stars to see,
Bread I dip in the river—
There's the life of a man like me,
There's the life for ever.

> Robert Louis Stevenson (1850—1894), 'The Vagabond', from *Songs of Travel.*

The king was in his counting house
Counting out his money;
The queen was in the parlour
Eating bread and honey;
The maid was in the garden
Hanging out the clothes,
There came a little blackbird
And snapped off her nose.

> *Tommy Thumb's Pretty Song Book* (c. 1744)

He took my father grossly, full of bread,
With all his crimes broad blown, as flush as May;
And how his audit stands who knows save heaven?

> William Shakespeare (1564—1616),
> *Hamlet,* III. iii. 80.

[On the Scotch]
'Their learning is like bread in a besieged town: every man gets a little, but no one gets a full meal.'

> Samuel Johnson (1709—1784), quoted Boswell's
> *Life,* vol. ii, p. 363. 18 Apr. 1775.

Who never ate his bread in sorrow,
Who never spent the darksome hours
Weeping and watching for the morrow
He knows ye not, ye heavenly powers.

> Translation of Goethe's *Wilhelm Meister's Apprenticeship,* bk. ii, ch. 13.

Buttyology Terminology

BREADTH—the width of a butty.
BUTTYTARIAN—one who lives on nothing but butties.

BUTTISEUR—an acknowledged expert buttyologist.
BUTTYHOLIC—a sandwich addict.

DO NOT FEED THE BUTTYTARIANS

BUTTIFULL—a surfeit of sandwiches.

BUTTYGLUTTY—a greedy butty eater.

BREADY-BYES—a sandwich supper.

CRUSTINESS QUOTIENT—the size and thickness of crust (important factor for denture wearers).

CONNY-ONNY—a Liverpool delicacy consisting of condensed milk on slices of bread and butter.

DOORSTEP—a very thick slice of bread or butty.

DUNK—to dip chunks of bread into soup, gravy etc.

EATIMOLOGY—the study of butty words and phrases.

EDI-BULL—a beefburger.

FLOUR-ARRANGER—a baker with artistic tendencies.

FRAB—Fellow of the Royal Academy of Buttyology.

GRANARY—a sort of home for grannies.

GUMPTION—what it takes to chew stale bread if you've had your teeth out.

GRED 'N' GUTTER—a ventriloquist's lunch.

ILL-BRED—a sick loaf.

JAWBREAKER—an extremely large butty.

JAMBOREE—a Liverpool kid's way of saying jam butty.

LONGICHEWED—a freshly-eaten French loaf.

MBE—Mighty Big Eater.

NEWCRUMBER—a fresh student at the Academy of Buttyology.

PASTA—a method of overtaking—as in 'We went pasta bloke on a motor-bike.'

SOLDIER—thin slices of toast used for dunking in the yolks of boiled eggs.

SELF-RAISING FLOUR—flour that has its own alarm clock.

WHEATMEAL—a chicken's dinner.

WHEATGERMS—what a stalk of wheat spreads when it sneezes.

Doddy's Crossword Puzzle for Brainy Buttyologists

1	2	3	4	5
2				
3				
4				
5				

YOU HAVE 30 SECONDS TO FILL
IT IN (PREFERABLY WITH A SHOVEL)
STARTING FROM *NOW.*

CLOOS: 1 ACROSS: BY TUT' (ANAG).
2 ACROSS: A WELSHMAN'S NAME FOR HIS MATE.
3 ACROSS: LORD SANDWICH'S INVENTION.
4 ACROSS: RHYMES WITH PUTTY.
5 ACROSS: GOOD NICKNAME FOR A GOAT?

1 DOWN: WHERE HONEY COMES FROM.
2 DOWN: FEMALE SHEEP.
3 DOWN: TO VEX, IRRITATE OR ANNOY.
4 DOWN: THEY COME AFTER BREAKFASTS AND LUNCHES.
5 DOWN: THE THREE ____ MEN.

DONE IT? THE ANSWERS ARE PRINTED UPSIDE-DOWN SO
YOU WILL HAVE TO STAND ON YOUR HEAD IF YOU WANT
TO SEE THEM.

CROSSWORD ANSWERS: 1 ACROSS *Butty.* 2 ACROSS *Butty.*
3 ACROSS *Butty.* 4 ACROSS *Butty.* 5 ACROSS *Butty.*
1 DOWN *Bees (B's).* 2 DOWN *Ewes (U's).* 3 DOWN *Tease (T's).*
4 DOWN *Teas (T's).* 5 DOWN *Wise (Y's).*

Index